Random Reflections

Brian Pondenis

BookLeaf
Publishing

India | USA | UK

Presentation by *BookLeaf Publishing*

Web: www.bookleafpub.com

E-mail: info@bookleafpub.com

ISBN: 9789363317727

First edition 2023

DEDICATION

Lovingly dedicated to Vivian and Calvin, the lights of my life. Never let anybody extinguish your flames of creativity.

ACKNOWLEDGEMENT

I thank a dear friend, J.P., for her encouragement in writing this.

Sunrise

As darkness fades and night takes flight
A new day dawns, with radiant light
The sky alight with hues of gold
As the sun begins to take hold

The world awakens with each new ray
And so begins another new day
From birds that sing and trees that sway
To oceans blue and fields of hay

The sun rises, a majestic sight
Filling the world with glorious light
And as it climbs higher in the sky
The day begins, and life goes by

So let us cherish each sunrise new
And all the wonders it brings in view
For every dawn is a chance to start
A day full of hope and joy and heart.

Glimmering Wings

Fluttering wings of vibrant hue
Graceful dancers, they are true
Butterflies, oh how they inspire
Filling hearts with sweet desire

Softly floating through the air
With beauty beyond compare
Rainbows caught within their flight
A stunning, breathtaking sight

From cocoons they are reborn
Metamorphosis, a journey worn
Emerging as a work of art
An emblem of life's fresh start

Delicate and fragile they seem
Yet, they endure, they dream
Flitting from flower to flower
Spreading love with every hour

Butterflies, a symbol of hope
Reminding us that we can cope
With change and transformation too
Like them, we can start anew

So let them dance, let them fly
As they paint the open sky
Butterflies, oh how they inspire
Filling hearts with sweet desire.

Two Wheels

Two spoked wheels
Tires humming on pavement
A rush of speed
And total excitement

From point A to B
Speedily
Wind racing through your hair *
As you race to get there

Maybe to a picnic,
Maybe to meet friends.
Could be off to school.
The fun never ends.

On a bright June afternoon,
The sprockets and gears click
A well-oiled chain
You get there quick

To a grassy park
Staying out til dark
Streetlights come on
And it's time to go

Tires pumped up for another day
A day in the sun, a day of fun
Riding, speeding all over town
Nothing could make this day go down.

Enjoy it while you can, because
Soon you will seek to trade
Two wheels for four
Always remember how
You used to explore
On two wheels.

*You should wear a helmet!

Six-Legged Soldiers

In the grass they scurry and crawl,
The ants, so busy, so small.
A million legs in motion,
Building homes with such devotion.

Their world is hidden from our sight,
A maze of tunnels, day and night.
In the blades of grass they thrive,
A community, so alive.

They gather food and tend to the young,
Their work is never truly done.
Each ant knows its role and place,
Together they create a bustling space.

Their tiny bodies, strong and tough,
Endure the heat, the rain, the rough.
In their world, each ant has worth,
A single worker, but part of the earth.

So let us not forget the ants,
Invisible heroes, always advance,
Their hard work keeps the grass green,
The unseen champions of the scene.

Summer Buzz

In the heat of summer,
The cicadas emerge
Their symphony of song
Is a chorus that surges

A buzz that fills the air
And echoes through the trees
Their rhythm pulses on
With a gentle ebb and breeze

Their wings, they shimmer
In the sun's warm light
As they hum and trill
Through the long, hot night

Oh, cicadas, how you sing
With such passion and zeal
A soundtrack to summer
That we can all feel

So let us bask in your melody
And soak up the lazy days
As you serenade us all
In your own unique ways.

Friends

A friend is a treasure, a gem so rare,
Whose presence in life brings joy and care.
A companion to walk with in times of need,
A confidante to share secrets and heed.

A friend is someone who lends an ear,
To listen, support, and offer good cheer.
They lift us up when we're feeling down,
And help us smile when we wear a frown.

A friend is a mirror, reflecting our soul,
A source of wisdom to help make us whole.
They guide us through life's twists and turns,
And share the lessons that they've learned.

A friend is a bond that cannot be broken,
A love so strong it will never be spoken.
They are the glue that holds us together,
Through all the storms of life, now and forever.

So cherish your friends, both near and far,
For they are the light that guides us like a star.
With them by our side, we can conquer all,
And stand tall and proud, through every fall.

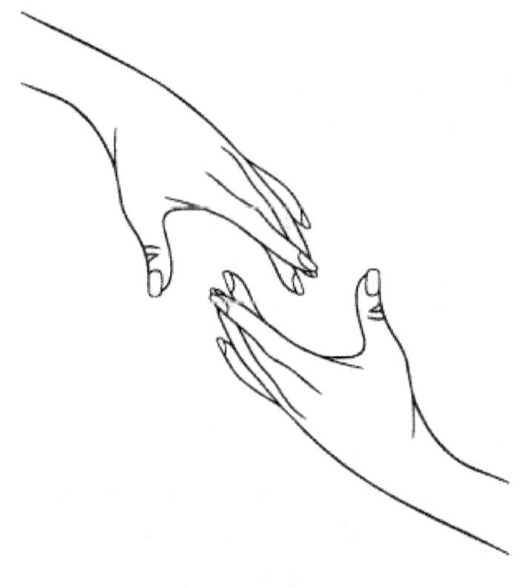

Sunny Days

Summer breeze, oh how you tease
Softly rustling through the trees
Caressing skin with gentle ease
As if a lover's touch to please.

Your warmth embraces all around
A soothing sound, a gentle sound
Whispering secrets, lost then found
A sweet symphony, heavenly bound.

The air is filled with scents divine
Wildflowers bloom, sweet berries shine
As you dance with grace, and unwind
A feeling of bliss, a peace of mind.

The sun shines bright, the sky is clear
A time of joy, a time of cheer
As you blow away all our fears
And chase away our every tear.

Summer breeze, you bring such delight
A feeling of freedom, a joyful flight
As we bask in your radiant light
And savor each moment, with all our might.

A Day at the Cafe

In a cozy cafe where time slows down,
I while away on a lazy day in town.
Coffee and espresso, their fragrant swirl,
Delighting my senses as flavors unfurl.

The sun shines bright, casting a golden hue,
Illuminating moments, both old and new.
A gentle breeze dances through the air,
Caressing my skin with a touch so fair.

People come and go, like fleeting dreams,
Each with their stories, like flowing streams.
Some lost in thought, others engaged in chatter,
The cafe a stage for lives to scatter.

Through the window pane, I watch the square,
Observing the world with a curious stare.
Faces passing by, a colorful parade,
In their footsteps, stories cascade.

The bustling city, a backdrop of life,
With joy and sorrow, love and strife.
Yet here I sit, in this haven of calm,
Absorbing the sights like a soothing balm.

I sip my coffee, lost in reverie,
As time unfolds, an exquisite tapestry.
The lazy day stretches, serenely sublime,
Wrapped in the rhythm of this tranquil rhyme.

In this cafe, a sanctuary I've found,
Where moments of solace and peace abound.
A respite from the chaos that surrounds,
Where lazy days become sweet resounds.

So let me linger, in this blissful repose,
As the world goes on, its story still grows.
In this cafe of dreams, I'll forever stay,
Watching people on the square, on this lazy day.

A Best Friend

A loyal friend with a wagging tail,
A bundle of joy that will never fail,
A creature of love with boundless heart,
A dog is a blessing from the very start.

They greet us with enthusiasm and glee,
As if every moment is a grand jubilee,
With their wet nose and soulful eyes,
They never fail to mesmerize.

They chase after sticks with utmost glee,
Or curl up at our feet so peacefully,
Their presence is a constant delight,
A source of comfort both day and night.

A dog's love is pure and true,
A bond that nothing can undo,
They are faithful companions until the end,
Four-legged family members, loyal friends.

So let us cherish these furry pals,
And love them with all our hearts and souls,
For they bring us joy beyond measure,
And make our lives all the more pleasurable.

Autumn Starts

Autumn, oh autumn, how you arrive,
With a soft rustle, the leaves take a dive,
From the trees that once stood tall and green,
Now they lay scattered, a beautiful scene.

The air is crisp, the breeze is cool,
The sun shines bright, a precious jewel,
As the days grow shorter, and nights get longer,
Nature's colors come alive, in shades much
stronger.

The sky turns orange, pink, and gold,
The hues of autumn, a sight to behold,
The trees dressed in their finest attire,
A show of beauty that never will tire.

The smell of pumpkin spice, and apple pie,
The taste of warm cider, a sweet lullaby,
Autumn is a season, like no other,
It fills our hearts, with joy and wonder.

As we watch the leaves fall, one by one,
We are reminded, that life must go on,
Like the cycle of seasons, we too must change,
Grow, and evolve, through life's endless range.

So let us embrace, this season so true,
And cherish the memories, that come anew,
For autumn, oh autumn, how you remind,
That beauty can be found, in every kind.

Shooting Star

I cannot write a better version of you,
For you are unique, there's no one like you,
In all the world, you stand apart,
A masterpiece, a work of art.

You are more than just flesh and bone,
You have a spirit that's all your own,
A heart that beats with passion and fire,
A soul that soars higher and higher.

Your words are like a gentle breeze,
That lifts the heart and calms the seas,
Your smile can light up any room,
And bring joy to those who meet your bloom.

You have the strength to face any strife,
And overcome the challenges of life,
You rise above trials that you face,
And emerge with grace, and a steady pace.

So do not wish for a better version of you,
For you are perfect, through and through,
Embrace yourself, just as you are,
And shine your light, like a shooting star.

A Broken Friend

Eyes that once shone bright with joy,
Now dimmed by a weight they can't avoid,
The light that once danced within them,
Now lost in sadness, a shadow within.

The tears that well up and overflow,
Revealing a depth of pain we cannot know,
A heart heavy with sorrow and despair,
With every blink, a silent prayer.

Sadness etched upon each line and crease,
Eyes that speak a language of grief,
A story told without a sound,
A pain too great to be unbound.

Yet within those eyes lies a strength,
A resolve to face whatever comes at length,
A courage to keep on despite the pain,
To embrace the light and find hope again.

So if you see sadness in someone's eyes,
Remember that there is more to the guise,
For within that person lies a heart so true,
A soul that shines with the light of a thousand
hues.

The Nightmare Tree

The heart of darkness, where nightmares roam
free
Stands a tree, twisted, gnarled as can be
Its branches stretch out like bony fingers
Reaching for those who dare to linger.

Its leaves are withered, its bark is rough
This nightmare tree is more than enough
To scare even the bravest of souls
And fill their minds with fearful goals.

In the dead of night, it casts its spell
Creating horrors that make hearts swell
Monstrous creatures emerge from its trunk
In a frenzy of fear, hearts nearly sunk.

This tree's a symbol of terror and dread
An embodiment of all that's unsaid
A warning to those who wander too far
Into the realm of the nightmare's scar.

So beware of the nightmare tree, my friend
Its power over you may never end
Once you've encountered its twisted form
Your dreams will be forever transformed.

Our Feline Friends

Graceful and sleek, with eyes so bright,
Cats prowl and wander through the night.
With a regal poise and a curious gaze,
They slink through the world in mysterious
ways.

Silent and stealthy, they prowl through the
house,
Playing with toys and chasing a mouse.
Curling up on a warm, cozy lap,
They purr and snooze in a content nap.

Independent creatures, with personalities unique,
Cats are full of surprises, never meek.
From a playful kitten to a wise old cat,
Their loyalty and love is never flat.

With their soft fur and their gentle purrs,
Cats bring joy and comfort to all they prefer.
As they stretch and yawn, settling in for the
night,
We know that with cats, everything will be
alright.

Sunset

Up in the sky, so high and bright,
The sun shines down with all its might.
The birds all sing, the bees all buzz,
As flowers bloom with colors that wows.

The wind blows gently through the trees,
As children play and run with glee.
They laugh and shout, and jump and dance,
Their joy and energy hard to chance.

But when the day comes to an end,
The sun sets low, and round the bend,
The moon comes out to light the night,
And stars twinkle, oh so bright.

So snuggle up, and close your eyes,
And dream of birds, and bees, and skies.
For tomorrow, when you wake anew,
The world awaits, just for you!

Guiding Light

Wishing star up in the sky,
Twinkling light that catches my eye.
I close my eyes and make a plea,
Hoping my wish will come to be.

You shine so bright, so far away,
Yet I can see you every day.
A beacon of hope that guides me through,
As I navigate life, unsure what to do.

I make a wish upon your light,
Hoping it will bring me delight.
Perhaps it's love that I desire,
Or success to which I aspire.

Oh wishing star, please hear my plea,
And grant my wish, so I may be free.
To chase my dreams and reach my goal,
With you as my guide, my heart and soul.

So keep on shining, bright and true,
And know that I will always pursue
My hopes and dreams, with you in sight,
Dear wishing star, my guiding light.

1986

Late nights with Dad were always grand
With stars above and telescope in hand
We'd search the skies for Halley's Comet
And marvel at the constellations we met

But it wasn't just stargazing we'd do
There were fireflies to catch and candy bars too
We'd sit on the porch and watch them blink
While Dad would tell stories that made me think

He'd speak of distant galaxies and more
Of black holes and supernovas galore
And though I was young, I'd understand
For dad had a way of making it grand

Late nights with Dad were always the best
Filled with wonder, adventure, and rest
As we lay under the stars with our candy bars
Watching the glowing red body of Mars

Memories we'd treasure for years to come
Of late nights with Dad and all the fun
Of fireflies and stars and Halley's Comet
And the love that Dad poured out - I'll never
forget.

The Moonlit Moth

In the still of the night,
When the moon shines bright,
A creature takes to flight,
Its wings a verdant sight.

The Luna Moth, a beauty rare,
With emerald wings that flare,
Drawn to the moon's soft glare,
It flutters without a care.

Its allure in the moonlight,
A mystical, enchanting sight,
As it dances in the night,
A creature of pure delight.

Its wings a vibrant hue,
A shade of green so true,
Reflecting light anew,
As it dances through the dew.

Luna Moth, how you captivate,
With your green wings so great,
Drawn to the moon's gentle fate,
A beauty we cannot debate.

May you forever dance and fly,
In the moon's celestial sky,
A creature we can't deny,
Your beauty will never die.

Moonlight

Beneath the moonlight's sorrowful glow,
I feel the weight of my heart's woe.
Its light, so cold and pale and bright,
Reveals the loneliness of the night.

It casts a mournful, eerie spell,
On all that lies beneath its swell,
A glimmering veil of silver tears,
That masks the pain and hides the fears.

In its beams, I see my reflection,
A broken soul with no direction,
Lost in the endless sea of pain,
Yearning for the light to shine again.

But all that's left is the moon's embrace,
A solitary beauty in a desolate space,
A haunting presence in the dark of night,
A reminder of the emptiness of life.

So I sit and watch the moon's slow rise,
And let its melancholy touch my eyes,
For in its anemic light I find,
A kindred spirit of the wounded mind.

New Beginnings

From ashes born anew,
The phoenix spreads its wings,
Once broken, now renewed,
In flight, it sweetly sings.

Through trials and through pain,
It faced the darkest night,
Yet still it would remain,
And rise towards the light.

Though grounded for a time,
Its spirit never died,
For it had faith sublime,
And hope that it would glide.

Now soaring to the skies,
It leaves behind the past,
Its strength a grand surprise,
Its beauty meant to last.

So let us learn from this,
And rise from where we fell,
For in us lies the bliss,
Of flying high and well.

Hummingbird

A hummingbird, a marvel in flight,
Careless and free, a radiant sprite,
With wings that flutter, a rapid embrace,
A ballet of beauty, a dance of grace.

Hovering like a bee, you sip from the bloom,
Unfazed by the world, a creature of plume,
Your iridescent feathers catch the sun's kiss,
A moment suspended, pure and bliss.

A symphony of colors, a vibrant display,
As you flit and dart in a magical ballet,
Collecting sweet nectar, a life-giving prize,
You weave through the garden, a
masterpiece in the skies.

Eyes aglow with wonder, you capture our
gaze,
A fleeting enchantment, a sunlit maze,
Your heart beats wild, a rhythm untamed,
In the realm of the flowers, your essence
proclaimed.

Oh, hummingbird, messenger of the air,
You teach us to live without a care,
To embrace each moment, to fly on a whim,
A lesson of life, from your delicate hymn.

You drink so delicately from the flowers,
Reminding us of your wings' powers
In the light of the orange dawn
Your wings hover forever on.

So let us take heed of your delicate flight,
A reminder to live in the present's light,
To savor the sweetness life has to give,
And in the dance of existence, truly live.

A new day, a brand-new light
As your wings soar and our hearts beat
We take stock of our lives
Whether love, loss, or plight.